REDUCING GLOBAL WARMING

Molly Mack

PowerKiDS
press

New York

Published in 2017 by The Rosen Publishing Group, Inc.
29 East 21st Street, New York, NY 10010

First Edition

Editor: Theresa Morlock
Book Design: Reann Nye

Photo Credits: Cover (background), pp. 1–24 (background) jwblinn/Shutterstock.com; cover (map), pp.1–24 Buslik/Shutterstock.com; cover (top), p. 1 Tatiana Grozetskaya/Shutterstock.com; cover (bottom) Armin Rose/Shutterstock.com; p. 4 chuyuss/Shutterstock.com; p. 5 Nickolay Khoroshkov/Shutterstock.com; p. 6 Elenamiv/Shutterstock.com; p. 7 Yorkman/Shutterstock.com; p. 8 Ethan Daniels/Shutterstock.com; p. 9 FloridaStock/Shutterstock.com; p. 10 Efired/Shutterstock.com; p. 11 Barcroft Media/Getty Images; p. 13 Pamela Moore/E+/Getty Images; p. 15 hans engbers/Shutterstock.com; p. 16 Eugene Suslo/Shutterstock.com; p. 17 Stephen Bures/Shutterstock.com; p. 18 Henrik Winther Andersen/Shutterstock.com; p. 19 EvgenySHCH/Shutterstock.com; p. 21 Jamie Grill/Getty Images; p. 22 Peter Cade/Photographer's Choice/Getty Images.

Cataloging-in-Publication Data

Names: Mack, Molly.
Title: Reducing global warming / Molly Mack.
Description: New York : PowerKids Press, 2017. | Series: Global guardians| Includes index.
Identifiers: ISBN 9781499427547 (pbk.) | ISBN 9781499429350 (library bound) | ISBN 9781508152767 (6 pack)
Subjects: LCSH: Global warming–Juvenile literature. |Global warming–Prevention–Juvenile literature.
Classification: LCC QC981.8.G56 M34 2017 | DDC 363.738'74–dc23

Manufactured in China

CPSIA Compliance Information: Batch #BW17PK: For Further Information contact Rosen Publishing, New York, New York at 1-800-237-9932

CONTENTS

A CHANGING PLANET

Whether it's hot, cold, rainy, or dry, the many plants and animals that live on Earth have learned to survive in its conditions. However, over the last 100 years or so, Earth's temperature has begun to rise too quickly. This **phenomenon** is known as global warming.

Global warming means more than rising temperatures. It causes serious problems, and some plants and animals are dying because of it. People are the leading cause of global warming. To slow it down, we must act now.

Global warming is caused by human activity. It's our responsibility to act before it's too late.

THE GREENHOUSE EFFECT

The glass walls of a greenhouse let in sunlight and trap heat, which warms the inside. Gases in Earth's **atmosphere** cause it to trap heat like a greenhouse.

The sun's rays pass through Earth's atmosphere. Most of the sunlight is **absorbed** into Earth's surface. Some of the **energy** bounces back in the form of heat. Greenhouse gases keep some of the heat from leaving the atmosphere. When too much heat is trapped near Earth's surface, the planet's temperatures rise.

CONSERVATION CLUES

A greenhouse gas is a gas in the air, such as carbon dioxide, that absorbs heat.

We need some greenhouse gases to keep our planet warm. This is called the greenhouse effect. Without it, Earth would be too cold to support life.

CLIMATE CHANGE

You've probably heard the phrase "climate change." Climate change is linked to global warming.

Some changes in Earth's climate are natural. **Glaciers** show evidence, or signs, that Earth's climate has changed slowly over thousands of years. Scientists believe global warming is causing the climate to change more quickly than it would be naturally. This is bad news for the world's plants and animals. Today, the climate is changing more quickly than they can **adapt**, and many are suffering.

Animals and plants that only live in one kind of **habitat** or eat a special diet are most at risk of being hurt by climate change. If their habitat or food source disappears, they will disappear, too.

EFFECTS OF GLOBAL WARMING

Warmer temperatures might sound appealing if you live in a cold, snowy climate. However, for animals such as penguins and polar bears, global warming is causing their icy homes to melt faster than they can adapt to the changes.

A large amount of people live near oceans. Ocean levels rise as glaciers melt. This puts both animals and humans in danger. Towns and cities along the coast are in danger of flooding. Land is disappearing as water covers it. Flooding and storms have already forced people from their homes.

CONSERVATION CLUES

The city of Venice, Italy, has canals, or waterways, running through it instead of streets. What will happen to the city as water levels rise?

Global sea level has risen about 8 inches (20.3 cm) since 1880. By 2100, it could very well rise another 1 to 4 feet (0.3 to 1.2 m). All that water has to go somewhere, and it's spilling over into communities around the world.

HELPING OUT

The leading cause of global warming is human activity. Producing the electricity used to heat and cool our homes also produces greenhouse gases. One way to slow global warming is to **conserve** energy, which means limiting how much we use.

Always turn off your lights, TVs, and computers when you're not using them. Think carefully before using a heater or air conditioner. When you save energy, you help save the **environment** from the dangerous effects of global warming.

CONSERVATION CLUES

Many companies are building refrigerators, stoves, dishwashers, and washing machines to be more energy efficient. That means these tools use less energy to get the job done.

It uses less energy to make a product from recycled materials than it does to make something new. Recycle your cans, bottles, and paper whenever you can. It's an easy way to help the environment!

THE TROUBLE WITH CARS

When cars burn fuel, they release chemicals and pollution into the air. This contributes to global warming. Scientific reports show that for every gallon (3.8 L) of gasoline burned, a car releases 24 pounds (10.9 kg) of greenhouse gases into the air. How can you help? Use cars less!

Buses, trains, and subways carry many passengers at once, which reduces the number of cars on the road. This leads to fewer greenhouse gases and less pollution. Walking and riding your bike produces no greenhouse gases at all.

CONSERVATION CLUES

Emmissions from cars and trucks make up about 20 percent of the greenhouse gas emmissions in the United States.

Some companies are building cars that use less energy. Electric cars are friendlier to the environment.

ENVIRONMENTALLY FRIENDLY ENERGY

People have started trying to find renewable sources of energy. A renewable resource is something that's replaced after you've used it, such as wind and sunlight. Renewable energy doesn't produce greenhouse gases, so it's a good solution to the problem of global warming.

Solar power is energy that comes from the sun. People use solar power to heat their homes and water. Wind power is another renewable resource. Wind **turbines** catch the wind and turn it into electricity.

More than 40 percent of the energy used in Denmark is supplied by wind power. Many countries are turning to wind power to replace fossil fuels as an energy source.

WHAT'S A CARBON SINK?

The most common greenhouse gas is carbon dioxide. Carbon dioxide is released when fuels such as wood, coal, or gasoline are burned. We even give off carbon dioxide when we breathe. However, nature helps us. Earth's oceans, plants, and soil are carbon sinks—they take in and store carbon dioxide.

Unfortunately, people are cutting down forests around the world to clear space for homes and buildings. Without forests to protect us, global warming will occur even faster. We need to conserve trees to protect all the living creatures that depend on them to take in carbon dioxide and release oxygen.

CONSERVATION CLUES

Deforestation is clearing an area of trees. If deforestation continues at its current rate, there won't be any rain forests on Earth 100 years from now.

Earth's trees are an important resource. We must take care not to waste them.

A GLOBAL PROBLEM

Global warming is happening everywhere. Greenhouse gases produced in one country enter the air and affect environments all over the world. Countries must join together to fight global warming.

Highly **developed** nations like the United States produce more greenhouse gases than smaller countries. We can lead by example when we conserve energy and use renewable energy sources. Global warming is a global problem, and it needs a global solution. It's everyone's job to pitch in to stop global warming before it's too late.

CONSERVATION CLUES

Every year, enough plastic is thrown away to circle Earth four times!

Think about all the energy your family uses in a day, whether it's through your TV, computer, phone, or family car. What are some ways your family can cut back on how much energy you use?

PART OF THE SOLUTION

Today, people are coming up with creative ways to conserve energy. Many states, such as California, Hawaii, and New Jersey, have passed laws to reduce creation of greenhouse gases. Companies are creating energy-efficient machines. Many people choose to walk and bike instead of using cars.

You can be part of the solution too. Look for ways to use less energy in your everyday life. Talk to your family about conserving energy in your home. The more people understand about the problem, the easier it'll be to fix.

GLOSSARY

absorb: To take in.

adapt: To change in order to live better in a certain environment.

atmosphere: The gases surrounding a planet, such as earth.

conserve: To keep something from harm and not waste it.

developed: The state of having many cities and businesses.

energy: The power to do work.

environment: The natural world around us.

glacier: A slowly moving mass of ice formed by snow that piled up in layers over many years.

habitat: The natural home for plants, animals, and other living things.

phenomenon: A fact or event that is observed.

turbine: An engine with blades that are caused to spin by pressure from water, steam, or air.

INDEX

WEBSITES

Due to the changing nature of Internet links, PowerKids Press has developed an online list of websites related to the subject of this book. This site is updated regularly. Please use this link to access the list: www.powerkidslinks.com/glob/warm

J 363.73
MACK, MOLLY